Design Management in Design Companies of Mexico City

ARTIUX

Copyright © 2016 Artiux
All rights reserved.
ISBN: 1535581468
ISBN-13: 978-1535581462

Dedications

To my beloved daughters, Alanna & Astrid

Contents

Acknowledgments v
Introduction vii
Description of the study 1
The interviews 4
   3indesign 5
   Diseño y Publicidad Mexicana 9
   Soluciones de Comunicación 13
   X Design 17
   Ysunza-Santiago Comunicación Visual 21
The shipments 24
   Carbono Consultores 25
   Figura 7 Despacho Creativo 29
   Sol Consultores 33
The phone call 37
   Dimensión 38
From the magazine articles 41
   Design Bureau 42
   Jota Erre Diseñadores 46
   TD2 49
Conclusions 52
Bibliography 61

Acknowledgments

To Antonio Pérez Iragorri Director of *a! Diseño* magazine, for his immediate authorization to consult from their copies all the information that was me useful in this project when barely started. Me too I like your interest in design business.

To Gerardo Clavel de Kruyff, Alfonso Aguilar Jiménez, Héctor Aguilar, and Zaira Torres Ambríz, Professors of the *Facultad de Arte y Diseño de la UNAM* [Faculty of Art and Design UNAM], who showed great interest and skill in review this study and on provide stage directions so valuable. Gerardo, from your initial support this whole project took great shape and strength. Alfonso, your reflexive enthusiasm infected me needed to continue this idea to their highest limits. Hector, assertiveness with which you support this effort made me continue the way; you also perform a singular job. Zaira, your depth analysis pushed me to improve those details that are the most important aspects in a project. The advice and opinions of each one of you are truly excellent.

To Ricardo Espinosa Trejo, Cofounder of 3inDesign, for sharing the interview between espressos, a very enriching chatter about being a designer and an aroma of surrounding tobacco. I agree with you, talent is what matters.

To Jaqueline Pulido, Chief Executive Officer of *Diseño y Publicidad Mexicana* [Design and Publicity Mexican], for allowing me to enter that world so creative and colorful, and for your attention to the interview be conducted in the most favorable environment, designing. An honor me feel your subsequent in your great team.

To Mercedes Charles Creel, Chief Editorial Officer of *Soluciones de Comunicación* [Communication Solutions], for giving me such valuable space when I most needed it. On seeing the passion with which you collaborated in this study, I continued looking for that energy until I find it completely.

To Pilar Muñoz, Chief Creative Officer of *X Design*, for inviting me with encouragement to continue insisting on doing what I like and what I want to achieve. You know how to make feel and lead to people.

To Enriqueta Santiago, Cofounder of *Ysunza Santiago Comunicación*

Visual [Ysunza Santiago Visual Communication], who together with Carlos Ysunza showed me some of the processes that arising from their great work throughout the interview. It is true professionalism is large part of project.

To Roberto Peralta, Chief Executive Officer of *Carbono Consultores* [Carbono Consultants], for giving me his much needed feedback and valuable comments. Generously sharing your knowledge and experience is what it sows the enterprising spirit in business.

To Ricardo Betanzos, Director of *Figura 7 Despacho Creativo* [Figure 7 Creative Office], he showed continued and great interest in the progress of this project. You're right, attention, patience and willingness to work makes you stand out.

To Enrique Saavedra, Owner of *Sol Consultores* [Sol Consultants], by repeatedly reading the interview, take the initiative to collaborate with some recommendations on the approach to some questions, and offer such valuable concepts. Yes, I will continue to insist strongly on the recognition of our profession.

To Mariana Moreno, Junior Designer of *Dimensión* [Dimension], she although so just they had the agenda and supporting their office, gave me the time needed for complete the interview keeping the headset on working hours. I like them offices in favor of the profession.

To Carlos González Nacif, Chief Executive Officer of *Design Bureau*. To Jorge Reyes Villalobos, Chief Executive Officer of *Jota Erre Diseñadores*. To Rafael Treviño, Chief Executive Officer of *TD2*. Those who expressed me to agree with Mr. Iragorri authorization to obtain information from the study of the copies of the magazine *a! Diseño*, where they are interviewed.

To my two daughters for their love, support and comprehension during realization of this project, which represents the beginning of the professional challenge of my career.

Thanks to you all for taking time out of their busy schedules. I want you to know that left a valuable mark on these pages. I really appreciate this of you.

Success in business does not come by itself, it is achieved by bringing the required combination and calculate its dose to keep expanding it

Introduction

This study pursuing the following objectives, know how these kinds of companies project management for the success of your business, how intervenes the use of briefing in a project, and how to determine whether the project was successful, on what refers to properly describe the design project management process, on the other hand, to check how these three parts of the process mentioned are directly articulated to the joint development of the three main disciplines that cause achieve success in business, that is, administration, marketing, and design, which are encompassed as general business process of a company.

It was made to those type of companies that can best provide a greater contribution to the objectives it seeks to publicize, design firms. Describing a project between an expert company in performing design projects and a corporate customer. Companies that were enthusiastic in collaborating in this study and had little to interact with their client. The study is based on design projects that were carried out at different firms in different fields of business each one.

Performance where it is intended:

For the design projects management process:

In the projection of administration: Observe how they define their goals, which determines the profile of the company reflects its structural strength and shows its projection to the market. (Where the posture of his administration is highlighted and marketing and design is reflected.)

In the use of briefing: Notice how is it extremely important with respect to market research and the projection of the company, the description of the design requirements that are taken to generate the right product or service. (Where the proposal of his design is highlighted and administration and marketing is reflected).

In the project's success: To understand on what basis to determine if the result of the project was successful for the office, his client, and the market, which would demonstrate their effectiveness. (Where the approach of his marketing is highlighted and design and management is reflected).

For the success of overall project business: Showing how act together, which by observation seem to be the three main disciplines of the overall project business, which can offer how to properly build a company so that it has a strong structure that is needed to stay in business, develop the commercialization skills to be accepted a greater extent by the target market and achieve the communication qualities with the expected effect the consumer chooses.

If you have a dream move to achieve it, then supports with what flows to him and build it so great that best meets its goal

Description of the study

The study presented here is an interview about business case in retrospect, it was performed to a composite sample of twelve design companies in Mexico City. Five of them were consulted directly in their offices, three of them indirectly through e-mail, also three more obtaining relevant information from specialized magazine articles, and one for conversation phone call as the best sources for gather information.

The study is based on 25 semi-structured questions included into three sections, each one with a purpose:

First, know the general information of the company to know in which bases its success and its future projection. That evidence aspects mainly their management process.

Second, analyze the design process management around a specific project and get to know their development through the briefing. That evidence aspects mainly their design process.

Third, make an assessment to the mobility of the company, customer engagement and project outcome. That evidence aspects mainly their marketing process.

These are the questions:

ARTIUX

Information and company profile

"What is the name of the office?"
"What is the philosophy of the office?"
"What is your mission?"
"What is your vision?"
"What is your age?"
"What is your number of personnel?"

To meet the objectives that projected in the industry, the profile that places it in the market, and managerial skills directing the project.

Requirements of the design project

"What is the name of the study project?"
"What was the objective of the project?"
"What was the method used to achieve the project?"
"What is the project concept?"
"What was the factor that caused the project?"
"Who developed the project requirements?"
"Who suggested the general concept?"
"Who defined the final concept?"
"Was there external support in realization of the project?"
"How many regular meetings were?"
"How long did the design process?"

To show requirements and market projection, development of project requirements, and product qualities.

Project evaluation

"The briefing was considered as a strategy in business design?"
"To promote the design profession was conducive to maintaining a differential advantage?"
"What activity highlighted for greater visibility, presence and penetration for this project in the design industry?"
"Philosophy of the firm was emphasized to explain the concept of the project?"
"Managers gave due importance to the brief?"

"The company considered design as a differential advantage?"

"The client appreciated the advantages that professional design services bring to your company?"

"Was it successful project outcome?"

To appreciate the effects it brings advantages to the company, assess implementation of the project design and know their results in the market.

This study is structured around the design project management process of (Bruce et al., 1999).

Overall, this study aims to document the value offered a proper design project management process, the importance of use of the brief, and its relationship to the main disciplines for success of a company.

No matter how many times you try or how much people deny you, but the moment you get up and affirm them

The interviews

"I think that entrepreneurs should evaluate more design work and its benefits that certainly deliver growth to their companies"

Ricardo Espinoza

3indesign

Mexico City, San Pedro de los Pinos area, Sanborns coffee. Interview with Ricardo Espinoza. Case Study: "Enrique Covarrubias Portfolio."

Information and company profile

"What is the name of the office?"
"*3indesign.*"
"What is the philosophy of the office?"
"Into *3indesign* we think do our job well is to provide the maximum effort and quality to every project in which we participate, reflected in the way of running business without losing sight of the objective of the client."
"What is your mission?"
"We are a company specialist in web design that offers solutions on multimedia tools and interactive media with the premise of serving the customer always well carrying out our small goals set."
"What is your vision?"
"Be one of the best web design agencies in Mexico participating in the market with global quality standards."
"What is your age?"
"We started in 2000."
"What is your number of personnel?"
"We are four members in the office and we have 4 external elements."

Requirements of the design project

"What is the name of the study project?"

"Enrique Covarrubias Portfolio."

"What was the objective of the project?"

"Broadcast international portfolio."

"What was the method used to achieve the project?"

"By recommendation of a client and subsequently agree with our quality of work."

"What is the project concept?"

"Design website."

"What was the factor that caused the project?"

"Having international presence to accomplish more work outside Mexico."

"Who developed the project requirements?"

"Both. The client offered their requirements and we help them give guidance trying to cover essential objectives rationally, it is important to listen to customers."

"Who suggested the general concept?"

"The client requested a breadth and impact design so that it perceived all over the world."

"Who defined the final concept?"

"Both. We present the proposals, the decision was left to the customer and the final solution; we did."

"Was there external support in realization of the project?"

"Yes, of the programmer."

"How many regular meetings were?"

"About eight meetings more constant contact by e-mail or Messenger that is faster."

"How long did the design process?"

"Approximately four months from project conceptualization."

Project evaluation

"The briefing was considered as a strategy in business design?"

"Yes, specifically to maintain a feedback relationship that was much needed to realize the project objectively."

"To promote the design profession was conducive to maintaining a differential advantage?"

"Yes, on the one hand design competitions were a great incentive for us, despite the rules of the jurors that make us more competitive. We like to measure ourselves because competition makes us grow and that drives us to maintain advantages over our competitors, on the other hand, to the market and for choosing this project."

"What activity highlighted for greater visibility, presence and penetration for this project in the design industry?"

"Our website, takes good care of the customer relationship maintaining contact with the network of people who recommends and some specialized magazines."

"Philosophy of the firm was emphasized to explain the concept of the project?"

"Yes, ever since the project began. Photographers, architects and large companies looked after much quality in all aspects, a quality of *3indesign*, is the main reason why which they hired us."

"Managers gave due importance to the brief?"

"Yes to some extent. Since the main objectives were considered, these were followed and the client was coupled, then the client was able to add some, but not changed."

"The company considered design as a differential advantage?"

"Yes. When our client asked us quality in the project was because was seeking to obtain great advantages of Web Design in a highly competitive environment like the Internet, especially for interactive we will emphasize its benefits."

"The client appreciated the advantages that professional design services bring to your company?"

"Yes, very well. The relationship with Enrique was in 2001 and continued working with him is much work and yes, valued what we did. Generally the clients we have also appreciate. Toward the market, I think that entrepreneurs should evaluate more design work and its benefits that certainly deliver growth to their companies."

"Was it successful project outcome?"

"For us much, for the customer who has won contracts in Germany, England, Spain and Maxim magazine following the creation of your site, it appears that too, although has expressed to us not convinced the international success than expected." (Espinosa, 2008)

"Is always a pleasure to work with good clients, when things work well and they are happy there is a in & out"

Jaqueline Pulido

Diseño y Publicidad Mexicana

Mexico City, Chapultepec Morales area, *Diseño y Publicidad Mexicana* offices. Interview with Jaqueline Pulido. Case Study: "Napkins *Pétalo* Independence day."

Information and company profile

"What is the name of the office?"
"*Diseño y Publicidad Mexicana.*"
"What is the philosophy of the office?"
"Into *Diseño y Publicidad Mexicana* the way we work is much more to offer our customers high-impact messages; we do through design and quality on time."
"What is your mission?"
"Our principles include serving customers always good at what we do, how we do it and the true value that this represents."
"What is your vision?"
"Being in the place we deserve, retaining clarity about who we are and our portfolio, since the design is first otherwise."
"What is your age?"
"We started in September 2002."

"What is your number of personnel?"

"We are seven members. The growth of the firm has been wonderful over the years we have been working, prefer to lead a good administration that high growth."

Requirements of the design project

"What is the name of the study project?"

"Napkins *Pétalo* Independence day."

"What was the objective of the project?"

"Keeping preference objective market *Pétalo* brand Kimberly-Clark Mexico for national holidays."

"What was the method used to achieve the project?"

"By contact the customer with whom we have worked on several projects."

"What is the project concept?"

"Polyethylene packagings design 500 napkins."

"What was the factor that caused the project?"

"Search for better design proposal."

"Who developed the project requirements?"

"Initially Kimberly. It is a steady customer, there is much contact in each process design and ongoing projects and we have coupled well, we know the possible alternative solutions to the requirements of the company. Only for new projects performed a previous meeting."

"Who suggested the general concept?"

"Respecting the parameter of the main character, we suggest the sketches, they chose of our 10 design proposals that combined motifs between *talavera*, chili, sweet toys, and so on."

"Who defined the final concept?"

"The customer. Normally so with Kimberly, we design and they choose."

"Was there external support in realization of the project?"

"No, the type of solutions we develop as a team, always stay within our parameters and capacity."

"How many regular meetings were?"

"Four meetings. We always have a lot of movement in the office, sometimes come to the office managers in charge of the project, I'm also going there, and this time was no exception. We were here for meetings and in their offices."

"How long did the design process?"

"Seven days, performance on the project was giving evolutionarily, working fast and with quality, with good proposals focused on what customers demand and always delivering on time."

Project evaluation

"The briefing was considered as a strategy in business design?"

"Yes, although in this project there were no, given the knowledge of the project characteristics previously."

"To promote the design profession was conducive to maintaining a differential advantage?"

"Yes, of course, the design is the first thing we highlight."

"What activity highlighted for greater visibility, presence and penetration for this project in the design industry?"

"Mainly the recommendation of our customers, of marketing managers who changing company with whom we have previously worked on different projects; the website and the magazine a! Diseño."

"Philosophy of the firm was emphasized to explain the concept of the project?"

"Yes, of course. It's something we always do and mentioned."

"Managers gave due importance to the brief?"

"Yes, it is serious, capable, professional and responsible people; I worked very happy with them."

"The company considered design as a differential advantage?"

"Yes."

"The client appreciated the advantages that professional design services bring to your company?"

"Yes, precisely for that reason they sought to design as a factor of innovation. Is always a pleasure to work with good clients, when things work well and they are happy there is a in & out."

"Was it successful project outcome?"

"The client was happy. Although there is no participation of this project in the market yet, good results are expected, merely for the season of his departure. For *Pétalo* Family, market tests that capture consumer acceptance exceeded expectations. The market share of the brand grew 1.7 percent points in 2006 compared to 2005, being the best performing brand in its segment. Both the packaging and promotions within the trends were accepted by the target audience very well." (Pulido, 2008)

"The design provides important added value is certainly true input know the advantages it gives. Both the design associations as design firms should promote the importance of design, making a social awareness among its members, customers, and staff"

Mercedes Charles Creel

Soluciones de Comunicación

Mexico City, Campestre Tlacopac area, *Soluciones de Comunicación* offices. Interview with Mercedes Charles Creel. Case Study: "Fuerte y Claro internal newspaper *Mexicana* Airlines."

Information and company profile

"What is the name of the office?"
"*Soluciones de Comunicación.*"
"What is the philosophy of the office?"
"Into *Soluciones de Comunicación* we are interested in developing a link with our clients to rightly interpret their needs to align communication with the strategic planning of the organization and that translates into effective results. As communications professionals, we work focused on client: our services and products will always express their needs. We strengthen our team in the daily life of institutional values: commitment, responsibility, quality, integrity, development and solidarity. As a result, we are confident that the care provided consistently reflects the spirit that animates our work. We offer personal attention by the partners, framed by a comprehensive view of communication processes that meet the business objectives of our clients. With the support of strategic alliances

with partner companies, we cover virtually all areas related to the communicative task."

"What is your mission?"

"We are a Mexican company specialized in offering solutions to their organizational communication needs. We provide high quality services in consulting, diagnostics and production, as well as dissemination and communication management and corporate image."

"What is your vision?"

"Be a leading company in our industry, providing our customers with efficient, flexible and timely responses. They form a mosaic that reflects the many facets of society. This diversity represents a challenge and an opportunity for continued growth: we must understand and respond to very different communication needs. We envision as the best office of integral communication solutions in Mexico."

"What is your age?"

"We started in 1998."

"What is your number of personnel?"

"We are twelve members here in the office. Sometimes we work with six free lances on average, depending on the project."

Requirements of the design project

"What is the name of the study project?"

"*Fuerte y Claro* internal newspaper *Mexicana* Airlines."

"What was the objective of the project?"

"Keep *Mexicana* Airlines personnel informed highlighting institutional values, integration and strategic objectives using the newspaper as a flexible media of timely information."

"What was the method used to achieve the project?"

"From the beginning of customer contact and so it has been until the last publication project that we carry nine years."

"What is the project concept?"

"Redesign of a leaflet aimed at personnel; we proposed a comprehensive magazine, which subsequently resulted in a tabloid newspaper for staff of the company. Ten pages and thirty average notes."

"What was the factor that caused the project?"

"Improving internal communication quality of the company with a media attractive accurate and timely. Results managers need to maintain efficient communication with more than 6,500 company employees across the continent."

"Who developed the project requirements?"

"The original requirements come from the client, we interpret your requirements and we gave our proposal, which handles two parts: editorial and design."

"Who suggested the general concept?"

"*Soluciones de Comunicación*."

"Who defined the final concept?"

"*Soluciones de Comunicación* and the client through a constant dialogue process of."

"Was there external support in realization of the project?"

"Do Not."

"How many regular meetings were?"

"Average eight meetings. Sometimes the whole process is done by mail."

"How long did the design process?"

"Three weeks of editorial work and design four days."

Project evaluation

"The briefing was considered as a strategy in business design?"

"Yes, it was essential."

"To promote the design profession was conducive to maintaining a differential advantage?"

"To any crisis first thing than is cut is internal communication, then the external, so promote the profession and image of the design is crucial, was essential. Yes kept advantages."

"What activity highlighted for greater visibility, presence and penetration for this project in the design industry?"

"Having website focus on human resources and design specialized magazines. Also the work of internal communication in companies, they recommended."

"Philosophy of the firm was emphasized to explain the concept of the project?"

"Yes, it was present in all actions of office, that is to say, honesty, quality; professionalism... as fundamental aspects of *Soluciones de Comunicación* considered and is present in all our projects."

"Managers gave due importance to the brief?"

"Yes, all."

"The company considered design as a differential advantage?"

"Yes, in most aspects. It depended on the type and size of the business, the niche, so on."

"The client appreciated the advantages that professional design services bring to your company?"

"I think sometimes yes and sometimes no. It depends on the client and his business vision might think that design is very important or is marginal. The design provides important added value is certainly true input know the advantages it gives. Both the design associations as design firms should promote the importance of design, making a social awareness among its members, customers, and staff."

"Was it successful project outcome?"

"It's a success. Annual assessments are made. People are happy, because *Fuerte y Claro* is considered as the primary media of communication into *Mexicana* Airlines; also is uploaded on the web in PDF." (Charles Creel, 2008)

"It's not easy, but I do not give up. My key thing is that I work for pleasure, for love what I do and I choose what I want to do"

Pilar Muñoz

X Design

Mexico City, Condesa area, *X Design* offices. Interview with Pilar Muñoz. Case study: "Annual report of social responsibility. Mexican Coca-Cola Industry."

Information and company profile

"What is the name of the office?"
"*X Design*."
"What is the philosophy of the office?"
"Our philosophy is that the customer is our guest, you have to feel at home; served and satisfied from start to finish the project."
"What is your mission?"
"Create the communication bridge between our clients and their audiences from the development of creative concepts and functional design that creates value. Integrating our customers in the process of creating strategic messages and then transforms them into tangible and successful projects that shape communication and strengthen the positioning of its brands."
"What is your vision?"
"Being the leading company in the creation of integrated corporate communication projects, whose value is based primarily on the ability to offer creative solutions designed to meet the needs of a constantly evolving market."

"What is your age?"
"I opened my office in 2002."
"What is your number of personnel?"
"Although we were only three people an administrative assistant, a designer and me. We are now seven."

Requirements of the design project

"What is the name of the study project?"
"Annual report of social responsibility. Mexican Coca-Cola Industry."
"What was the objective of the project?"
"Design a different report than in previous years."
"What was the method used to achieve the project?"
"An invitation to a Coca-Cola design competition."
"What is the project concept?"
"Design of internal report of Coca-Cola. That the report itself was a piece to remember where the values and actions of the company were translated."
"What was the factor that caused the project?"
"To say that for 80 years Coca-Cola has been part of Mexico."
"Who developed the project requirements?"
"*X Design* and Mexican Coca-Cola Industry. When reviewing in more detail the quality of information that was provided to us, we proposed a re-thinking of the whole project, where we present a new communication style changing the format, style of writing and photographic style to give place to final project."
"Who suggested the general concept?"
"Both we considered a series of questions about the meaning and value of opportunities found within the difficulties of life."
"Who defined the final concept?"
"The concept revolved around the global approach that Coca-Cola has to benefit and refresh every person with whom they interact. It is noteworthy that we present two proposals which the customer selected one. The report is raised such that, regardless of the sequence, the reader can access any page in random order, and the report provides data, a review, and an independent result of rest of the information."

"Was there external support in realization of the project?"

"Only Mexican Coca-Cola Industry. In order to answer the questions was necessary to live, go to a shelter, a bottling plant, at a training session at a water treatment plant and so forth and make a written and photographic record of it and then can transmit. So we managed a piece that works as a photographic witness with timely information from large portfolio of activities performed Coca-Cola around corporate social responsibility."

"How many regular meetings were?"

"Approximately ten."

"How long did the design process?"

"Four months."

Project evaluation

"The briefing was considered as a strategy in business design?"

"Today the design runs the risk of devalued owing to the oversupply of offices and independent designers, the shape of distinguish and provide much value added lay in the domain of integration of all study tools, evaluation and support each particular project requires."

"To promote the design profession was conducive to maintaining a differential advantage?"

"Yes, I always made it clear to my clients that did not intend to terminate projects to other firms, but knew they would surely have new projects to which could aspire. That worked very well, now we know that our customers are the greatest source of knowledge in each of their sectors, so that as a team with them, have managed to create successful projects that have given us awards at national and international level."

"What activity highlighted for greater visibility, presence and penetration for this project in the design industry?"

"Invitations to design competitions, one of the most important were for Coca-Cola where the first year I was in the second place and the following year won the contest and the right to design their annual social responsibility report. Similarly we get involved in projects for clients such as Nestle, Danone and Grupo Modelo. It's not easy, but I do not give up. My key thing is that I work for pleasure, for love what I do and I choose what I want to do. Many firms refuse to enter contests and they are right because often it is an unfair practice and sometimes unjust."

"Philosophy of the firm was emphasized to explain the concept of the project?"

"In *X Design* we understand that design is the visual expression of many disciplines together, one of them is marketing. Both taken properly, resulting in a sound communication based on strategic thinking. This will contribute to this creation value."

"Managers gave due importance to the brief?"

"As for the design that received the award, my opinion is that firstly, the project must meet the expectations and goals of communication arising from its inception and also if the result was recognized by a third party, then what better."

"The company considered design as a differential advantage?"

"I think the best customer experience was not only the result, but throughout the work process. We visualize each project with creativity, innovation and competitiveness to exceed their expectations."

"The client appreciated the advantages that professional design services bring to your company?"

"I am certain amount of projects per year, and sometimes are the same customers who return year after year after a satisfying experience. This practice created loyalty and commitment."

"Was it successful project outcome?"

"It was a very human report, figures, data and relevant information on each page, visually appealing, with balance between text and image; this earned him be recognized in ARC Awards (Annual Report Competition) award given in New York to the best of design in annual reports worldwide with a gold mention for best work in interior design and bronze mention for best picture." (Muñoz, 2008)

"Oneself as a designer must make them aware these advantages"

Enriqueta Santiago

Ysunza-Santiago Comunicación Visual

Mexico City, Condesa area, *Ysunza-Santiago Comunicación Visual* offices. Interview with Enriqueta Santiago. Case Study: "Jafra catalog Opportunities."

Information and company profile

"What is the name of the office?"
"*Ysunza-Santiago Comunicación Visual.*"
"What is the philosophy of the office?"
"In all our processes of creation, whether of images, strategies or concepts, we combine: aesthetics, function, significance, influence, effect, action, strength, certainty and power interacting propositively, resulted in better and more efficient solutions for our customers."
"What is your mission?"
"Offer our customers a comprehensive creative solution and a combined approach."
"What is your vision?"
"Search permanent new proposals that provide added value to the concept of communication; optimize resources through deep understanding of our disciplines; exceed the coverage that gives us more than 25 years of professional experience, continuing the constant training

and updating of our people through courses and diplomas in Mexico and abroad and maintain the procurement of equipment and latest generation technology to ensure total quality."

"What is your age?"
"We began in 1999."
"What is your number of personnel?"
"We are four members."

Requirements of the design project

"What is the name of the study project?"
"Jafra catalog Opportunities."
"What was the objective of the project?"
"Sales of cosmetic products."
"What was the method used to achieve the project?"
"At first by a professional recommendation subsequently by loyalty between client and at the office."
"What is the project concept?"
"Catalog design."
"What was the factor that caused the project?"
"Carry the Jafra products a higher position and increase sales."
"Who developed the project requirements?"
"The marketing department Jafra."
"Who suggested the general concept?"
"*Ysunza-Santiago Comunicación Visual.*"
"Who defined the final concept?"
"*Ysunza-Santiago Comunicación Visual.*"
"Was there external support in realization of the project?"
"Do Not."
"How many regular meetings were?"
"About seven meetings."
"How long did the design process?"
"Two months from project conceptualization."

Project evaluation

"The briefing was considered as a strategy in business design?"

"Yes, since was the entire project guide."

"To promote the design profession was conducive to maintaining a differential advantage?"

"Yes definitely. Promote the link was part of the sales strategy."

"What activity highlighted for greater visibility, presence and penetration for this project in the design industry?"

"The web page, diffusion by mail, contracts in journals and advertorials as *a! Diseño*."

"Philosophy of the firm was emphasized to explain the concept of the project?"

"Yes, as a sales tool."

"Managers gave due importance to the brief?"

"Yes, in general they always do."

"The company considered design as a differential advantage?"

"In some ways, in most did not, it need much education on what is this discipline in companies."

"The client appreciated the advantages that professional design services bring to your company?"

"Doing of nowhere was difficult. Oneself as a designer must make them aware these advantages, especially in a sales development as mentioned project."

"Was it successful project outcome?"

"Yes, to a year of the new design strategy have been implemented, Jafra has entrusted us apply the same to all of its preexisting publications and at the same time and for the first time, integrate it into ads in women's magazines and billboards. This due to the excellent results of the new catalogs, which have generated more than 35% increase in direct sales and increased market presence." (Santiago, 2008)

If you choose the design because it gives presence, meaning and functions what you buy, it is much better when you invest in it

The shipments

"The obligation of one agency is to use this tool and make them view their clients the importance of it"

Roberto Peralta

Carbono Consultores

Mexico City, provenance e-mail: Hipódromo Condesa area, *Carbono Consultores* offices. Interview with Roberto Peralta. Case Study: "Merger campaign *LexisNexis* and *Dofiscal*."

Information and company profile

"What is the name of the office?"
"*Carbono Consultores.*"
"What is the philosophy of the office?"
"Label us as a design firm or an advertising agency would be incomplete. The word that best defines our business is Consultants."
"What is your mission?"
"Our mission is comparable to that of a doctor. In our hands get all kinds of cases: some seriously injured, others require vitamins. We develop projects for clients to always provide a high quality service."
"What is your vision?"
"Always with the premise of to focus in customer and care of your brand."
"What is your age?"
"We started in 1997."
"What is your number of personnel?"
"We are twenty five members."

Requirements of the design project

"What is the name of the study project?"

"Campaign fusion *LexisNexis* and *Dofiscal*."

"What was the objective of the project?"

"Positioning the brands *LexisNexis* and *Dofiscal* as a new business consortium to their target audience."

"What was the method used to achieve the project?"

"*LexisNexis* contact with whom we had worked and knew the quality of our services."

"What is the project concept?"

"Consulting for *LexisNexis* and *Dofiscal* Campaign fusion."

"What was the factor that caused the project?"

"The union of two experts: *Dofiscal*, leader in the publishing market of specialized information for more than twenty five years and *LexisNexis* a leading global in fiscal solutions, legal and business information in the US. The publisher *Dofiscal* had a good position with the target audience (counters) and *LexisNexis* not; the idea or objective was to migrate the image and positioning *Dofiscal* to *LexisNexis*."

"Who developed the project requirements?"

"The project requirements were developed by the client, through filling a brief in which defined the objectives to communicate at their target. Once the agency got the brief was done a session work (debriefing) to define the ultimate objective."

"Who suggested the general concept?"

"*Carbono* team; who participated in this campaign, led by creative director together with the planner, creative copywriter, art director and designers."

"Who defined the final concept?"

"Was defined by the creative director his team and the client."

"Was there external support in realization of the project?"

"The project was supported by various participants, from the client and his team of communication, until the printers, who contributed ideas and opinions for the project, however, *Carbono* conducted throughout the conceptual and creative development consulting for the campaign."

"How many regular meetings were?"

"Approximately five meetings; beginning with the first filing and the rest to define the concept."

"How long did the design process?"

"Approximately two weeks from the development of creative platform to its application in a print and media (specialized magazines)."

Project evaluation

"The briefing was considered as a strategy in business design?"

"Yes. In a decade of achievements and growth has made the difference between giving solutions and place orders; between creating and designing only; between being consultants and contract manufacturers only. The brief is the starting point and the core of a communication project since there the objectives, scope, team that will participate, production resources, and so on, are defined. In the absence of this document is the risk of not achieving the desired goal of communication."

"To promote the design profession was conducive to maintaining a differential advantage?"

"Yes. The experience was our case, not only the previous accumulated, but the solid foundation to grow with our customer, be only one and share their needs, projects and goals."

"What activity highlighted for greater visibility, presence and penetration for this project in the design industry?"

"We define ourselves as a consulting agency in branding, marketing and communication, as we work with special care in customer service, creativity and results at set times for each project."

"Philosophy of the firm was emphasized to explain the concept of the project?"

"Yes. Although for this project took part only one area of the agency, we continue our philosophy branding + marketing + communication: strengthen and position the branding and then develop marketing strategies and communication."

"Managers gave due importance to the brief?"

"Yes. It is fundamental to a project, fortunately the people responsible for this project knows the importance of the brief. In this profession some clients omit develop a brief before starting a communication project because they have little time for launch. The obligation of one agency is to use this tool and make them view their clients the importance of it."

"The company considered design as a differential advantage?"

"We know well that every customer, every brand and every product is a different case: all require specialized treatment; therefore, we were sure that it was not a formula, was undoubtedly a matter of ideas."

"The client appreciated the advantages that professional design services bring to your company?"

"Yes, by our specialized divisions: *Carbono* Communications: research, branding, marketing; *Carbono* Interactive: web, marketing, solution; y *Carbono* Editorial: development, communication, tracking."

"Was it successful project outcome?"

"Yes, the first objective was achieved which was identified with *Dofiscal LexisNexis* and usher in the second stage of the campaign, which is to present its online tool with all the information accountants found in boards published by *Dofiscal*." (Peralta, 2008)

"Generally, companies that are directed to the final consumer are who putting more care in design and do see it as a competitive advantage as in the area of packaging and branding"

Ricardo Betanzos

Figura 7 Despacho Creativo

Mexico City, provenance e-mail: Portales area, *Figura 7 Despacho Creativo* offices. Interview with Ricardo Betanzos. Case Study: "Product Catalog Philips Consumer Electronics."

Information and company profile

"What is the name of the office?"
"*Figura 7 Despacho Creativo*."
"What is the philosophy of the office?"
"Put on the shirt of our customers is the phrase that best sums us up. We dedicate commitment and engagement in every project we do it makes us proud that our customers are satisfied to see the final result."
"What is your mission?"
"Giving our customers the best service and personalized attention, understanding their needs and offering graphic communication solutions according to market that target their products or services."
"What is your vision?"
"Being in the top 10 graphic design firms of Mexico and help improve the level of graphic design at the national level."
"What is your age?"
"We started in 2000."

"What is your number of personnel?"
"We are eight members."

Requirements of the design project

"What is the name of the study project?"
"Product Catalog Philips Consumer Electronics."
"What was the objective of the project?"
"Introduce to the final consumer the new line of LCD televisions flat relating it to a warm, elegant and sensual image."
"What was the method used to achieve the project?"
"There was already working relationship with the client. The initial contact was through the division of Philips Lighting."
"What is the project concept?"
"Design of electronic product catalog."
"What was the factor that caused the project?"
"There was already a catalog for this new line of products from Brazil, however not cover customer expectations and neither the Mexican market. The concept was sought tropicalizing."
"Who developed the project requirements?"
"Were elaborated and explained it for the marketing assistant."
"Who suggested the general concept?"
"Was suggested by the marketing director for the region; he communicated in writing by means of a brief."
"Who defined the final concept?"
"The final concept was defined between the client and graphic designer in charge of the project. Associate the product with an object of desire through sensual and attractive images, but elegant yet sophisticated. The last delivery was made on a cd with the final file to print and a dummy in color how the piece should be."
"Was there external support in realization of the project?"
"The cover photo was produced in Brazil, was published in Chile and sent it to Mexico directly to the office. The final impression was made through an external printer."
"How many regular meetings were?"
"Two in person and the others were by phone or e-mail."

"How long did the design process?"
"A month or so."

Project evaluation

"The briefing was considered as a strategy in business design?"

"Yes. We asked for a brief at customer. Most of the times are prompted for a brief to customer, although there are many who do not accustom use it."

"To promote the design profession was conducive to maintaining a differential advantage?"

"Even if it influenced to provide a better personalized service, it was not vital since the technology saved a lot of time and pulled one back in the design process."

"What activity highlighted for greater visibility, presence and penetration for this project in the design industry?"

"Really we not emphasized any activity in particular; mobility in the sector came from recommendations and contacts."

"Philosophy of the firm was emphasized to explain the concept of the project?"

"The firm's philosophy emphasized our work. The design philosophy of the very few times, I think is something should be done more often to give a better justification for what one does, but not all clients or projects lend themselves to that."

"Managers gave due importance to the brief?"

"Two briefs were generated; the first was not very defined and discarded after arming most of the catalog. A second was always tracked and respected, until finish project."

"The company considered design as a differential advantage?"

"It did so in this project. They have been few occasions when the client gives that value to the design. Generally, companies that are directed to the final consumer are who putting more care in design and do see it as a competitive advantage as in the area of packaging and branding."

"The client appreciated the advantages that professional design services bring to your company?"

"Yes. When the customer noticed the final result after a long design phase, corrections, sleeplessness, and so on and he saw your product framed or reinforced with good design, he realized it was worth it and that everything affects the image of your brand. All this leads to a better appreciation and acceptance of design services in Mexico."

"Was it successful project outcome?"

"The client was very happy and we received good reviews of it. Although it has not estimate until the catalog is in circulation and see that both worked and captured the attention of the consumer." (Betanzos, 2008)

"Most managers do not give importance to the briefing because they do not manage it in terms of identity, branding, and graphic design. Likewise, do not understand the benefits, risks, advantages, and disadvantages of the design or the various factors and consequences involved"

Enrique Saavedra

Sol Consultores

Mexico City, provenance e-mail: Guadalupe inn area, *Sol Consultores* offices. Interview with Enrique Saavedra. Case Study: "Karat Vodka."

Information and company profile

"What is the name of the office?"
"*Sol Consultores.*"
"What is the philosophy of the office?"
"In *Sol Consultores* we seek long-term relationships supporting our customers to create value for their brands beyond the functional benefits of their products and services. We believe consumers and functional, emotional, perceptual and experiential factors that influence our selection decisions and brand loyalty."
"What is your mission?"
"Providing brand and design solutions with a service approach highly creative and business."
"What is your vision?"
"Be the principal office of strategy and brand identity in Mexico."
"What is your age?"
"We started in 2002."
"What is your number of personnel?"
"We are twenty five members."

Requirements of the design project

"What is the name of the study project?"
"Karat Vodka."
"What was the objective of the project?"
"Increase participation and preference of the Karat brand with its target audience."
"What was the method used to achieve the project?"
"By references from a colleague and earlier clients."
"What is the project concept?"
"Product brand identity and design of bottle."
"What was the factor that caused the project?"
"Decreased sales; as results of market studies that showed a negative and confused perception towards the brand."
"Who developed the project requirements?"
"*Sol Consultores* and contracting firm."
"Who suggested the general concept?"
"*Sol Consultores*."
"Who defined the final concept?"
"A mix between research agency, the office, the client and consumers evaluated."
"Was there external support in realization of the project?"
"The project had several participants, from the client and their various engineering and brand teams. The research agency, to the various printers, illustrator, and photographer and bottle manufacturers were involved in opinions and ideas for the project, however, *Sol Consultores* conducted the conceptual, creative and production brand development."
"How many regular meetings were?"
"Approximately ten: planning, presentation of concepts, evaluation, research, bottle production, cap production, label printing, launching, among others."
"How long did the design process?"
"One year from conceptualization to launching."

Project evaluation

"The briefing was considered as a strategy in business design?"

"The preparation of the brief and the definition of the problem to be solved were the key elements of the design project."

"To promote the design profession was conducive to maintaining a differential advantage?"

"There are no major media directed towards potential customers that enable promote, disseminate and value the design industry. However it was due to seek the means to publicize the brand *Sol Consultores* to the customer."

"What activity highlighted for greater visibility, presence and penetration for this project in the design industry?"

"Ideally highlighted business magazines, but these do not pay attention to the design industry or not considered sufficiently relevant. It was necessary to use various means to disseminate differentiation and value of *Sol Consultores*. In our case excelled magazines, promotional, conferences, courses, postal, internet and direct marketing."

"Philosophy of the firm was emphasized to explain the concept of the project?"

"It is important to define philosophy. Be the philosophy of design office, or philosophy of the company / client or the concept as a basis to justify a solution. In our case, yes we did, and are the values and principles under which we operate or seek to establish: transparency, honesty, respect, teamwork, win-win, fairness, perseverance, service, personal growth, professional growth, other."

"Managers gave due importance to the brief?"

"Most managers do not give importance to the briefing because they do not manage in terms of identity, branding, and *graphic design*. Likewise, do not understand the benefits, risks, advantages, and disadvantages of the design or the various factors and consequences involved. For Karat Vodka, the brief was determined to dimension the objectives and technical limitations of the project."

"The company considered design as a differential advantage?"

"The design has many functions and its value changes depending on the circumstances and category of product, company or service. In some cases the value of design can be critical as in a perfume and virtually zero like a sack of flour. In the case of the vodka, where product differentiation is low, the role of design and bottle were keys to generate affective value."

"The client appreciated the advantages that professional design services bring to your company?"

"Customers appreciate the design differently and depending on various factors. In my opinion give little value to the design and designers compared to other professions or industries as doctors, lawyers, architects ... In this project valued at greater and lesser extent the design as a means of communication such as aesthetic element and an element of sales."

"Was it successful project outcome?"

"In terms of customer satisfaction, *La Madrileña* decided to continue working with *Sol Consultores* ascribing more projects, Karat Vodka increased its sales by 25% the first year, the product is now perceived as higher quality and is accepted by consumers with pride (despite its low price)." (Saavedra, 2008)

The design is a secret to the public eye. If you do not opt for it, it is because you have not discovered his gifts and how to apply them

The phone call

"We have a great experience to satisfy our customers with design needs required according to our performance areas"

Mariana Moreno

Dimensión

Mexico City, receiving the call Valle Escondido Colony, *Dimensión* offices. Interview with Mariana Moreno. Case Study "Catalog Platinum Members to *Fiesta* Hotels Rewards."

Information and company profile

"What is the name of the office?"
"*Dimensión*."
"What is the philosophy of the office?"
"As a strategic agency in graphic and corporate communications and marketing we have inspired by the word dimension (lat Dimensión Onís.), Which means: the importance or significance of something; as synonymous with faceted aspects of commitment, heart, creativity, strategy, success, future, perception, results service and value, they make us passionate, committed and professional in our work; we enjoyed greatly and we do it very well."
"What is your mission?"
"In dimension we have a great experience to satisfy our customers with design needs required according to our performance areas: corporate communications, strategic creativity, speech and copy, design pop material, editorial design, identity, illustration, marketing and retail branding."

"What is your vision?"

"We can proudly say that we have grown at a pace that surprises us ourselves. We always get with our work to seek recognition, merit that makes the firm soon gets bigger over time as well as we have been doing."

"What is your age?"

"10 years. We started in 1997."

"What is your number of personnel?"

-Data not specified.-

Requirements of the design project

"What is the name of the study project?"

"Catalog Platinum Members to *Fiesta* Hotels Rewards."

"What was the objective of the project?"

"Renew the image and catalogs that uses *Fiesta* Hotels to promote its services Platinum directed its target market, since its design after time, needed better acceptance."

"What was the method used to achieve the project?"

"For customer-office loyalty, because we have worked together on other projects."

"What is the project concept?"

"Redesign image and catalogs for Platinum Members."

"What was the factor that caused the project?"

"Noticeable disparity of the design of catalogs with the image that currently offer these Hotel. After given season, required to show a new image of catalogs that accompany the familiar image of the Hotel. Avoiding monotony, during the update that constantly is held."

"Who developed the project requirements?"

"*Dimensión*. Despite the ongoing work with the company, we took on the task of going to our brief."

"Who suggested the general concept?"

"*Dimensión*. We plan to make a substantial and noticeable change on an element in constant contact with their customers."

"Who defined the final concept?"

"*Dimensión*. We show the proposals and they dedicated themselves to choose the best adapted to their needs."

"Was there external support in realization of the project?"
"No, the whole design project was conducted by *Dimensión*."
"How many regular meetings were?"
"Just a pair. All contact was made by telephone and via mail."
"How long did the design process?"
"Exactly three weeks from receipt to delivery of the project."

Project evaluation

"The briefing was considered as a strategy in business design?"
"Yes, it was basic. As in every projects."
"To promote the design profession was conducive to maintaining a differential advantage?"
"Yes, of not doing so, would not have had the same success."
"What activity highlighted for greater visibility, presence and penetration for this project in the design industry?"
"The recommendation of the companies that know us and our work; we also finding customers through Internet dissemination, direct marketing and print media, always competing with quality:"
"Philosophy of the firm was emphasized to explain the concept of the project?"
"Yes, in our work we announced with her."
"Managers gave due importance to the brief?"
"No. In this project was needed them know their usefulness."
"The company considered design as a differential advantage?"
"Yes. They show interest because they know that something important of them would projected."
"The client appreciated the advantages that professional design services bring to your company?"
"Yes. They do not know much of design but have realized that it is a tool that makes being in the minds of consumers."
"Was it successful project outcome?"
"Yes. The client was happy." (Moreno, 2008)

Not only do what you love and love what you do because it benefits you, but also when it needs you

From the magazine articles

"If the idea of order and organization to customers is not transmitted, it is difficult to win major accounts. But to be seen and correctly perceived by customers, not enough to be a professional of the design, it is important to give the appearance of being. It is essential that customers stop to see us as those who do little drawings"

Carlos González Nacif

Design Bureau

Mexico City, source of information: a! Diseño Magazine. Design Bureau. Interview with Carlos González Nacif. Case Study "Antillano Rum."

Information and company profile

"What is the name of the office?"
"Design Bureau".
"What is the philosophy of the office?"
"Honesty, professionalism and dedication. Keep day to day a work environment and a quality of life that allows us to grow as people to provide good service."
"What is your mission?"
"Professionally and personally, always have something to offer."
"What is your vision?"
"To be clear, transparent. Offer services and products holding loyal relationships with our customers and suppliers to keep us full in business and in our personal relationships."
"What is your age?"
"16 years. We started in 1991."
"What is your number of personnel?"
"16 members."

Requirements of the design project

"What is the name of the study project?"
"Antillano Rum."
"What was the objective of the project?"
"Retain elements of the above but with a current communication presentation, keeping only the essence of the previous logo."
"What was the method used to achieve the project?"
"By Customer contact."
"What is the project concept?"
"Product redesign of."
"What was the factor that caused the project?"
"La Madrileña decided to turn 180 degrees to the image of one of its leading products."
"Who developed the project requirements?"
"Design Bureau."
"Who suggested the general concept?"
"Together with the customer we develop the profile and developed each of the illustrations were made by Rafael Barbabosa. Logo also was treated in different funds to strengthen the personality that the variant needed."
"Who defined the final concept?"
"The bottle was provided by the customer, being part of our work the label location, development and icon design under this, and wear the neck and the top of it. Rum White, Gold, and Aged handle different graphics solutions. Although under the same umbrella, vignettes they reflect different situations of the Antilles."
"Was there external support in realization of the project?"
"The graphics solution, the total redesign was held by Design Bureau."
"How many regular meetings were?"
-Data not specified.-
"How long did the design process?"
"The makeover elapsed and were making modifications to reach the final solution." -Data not specified.-

Project evaluation

"The briefing was considered as a strategy in business design?"

"Yes."

"To promote the design profession was conducive to maintaining a differential advantage?"

"Yes. Although the office born as an informal office, gradually has acquired a formal character. Today is a company with a corporate structure. This part is essential to the functioning of a design company; if the idea of order and organization to customers is not transmitted, it is difficult to win major accounts."

"What activity highlighted for greater visibility, presence and penetration for this project in the design industry?"

"The business name of the office is Buró de Diseño S.A. de C.V., although the trade name remained as Design Bureau. Our start was very peculiar, our first job was as an office freelance for Colgate Palmolive and practically from that moment we began working for big brands. In marketing positions usually there are many changes and we were fortunate to continue working with people they left Colgate Palmolive, some joined other big companies like Kimberly Clark Mexico and Comex, and continued to be our customers, all this helped us grow and diversify office projects."

"Philosophy of the firm was emphasized to explain the concept of the project?"

"Yes. But to be seen and correctly perceived by customers, not enough to be a professional of the design, it is important to give the appearance of being. It is essential that customers stop to see us as those who do little drawings."

"Managers gave due importance to the brief?"

"Yes in part. Although we also encounter often clients do not usually prepare a brief for the designer. Finally, all that talk about the lack of recognition of the professional design."

"Not at all. Every project design involves many more disciplines who believe customers. When it is possible to we bring to the office to know the design process and most times they are convinced the costs of our work."

"The client appreciated the advantages that professional design services bring to your company?"

"Already he valued and after seeing the results, did even more. Although they are becoming less, unfortunately there are still customers who summon to unpaid contests. From my point of view it does not seem fair that make us work that way; there are those who have not the foggiest idea what that implies what they are asking and with they we decided not to work, it does not make sense."

"Was it successful project outcome?"

"Yes. It's on the shelves. I love going to the supermarket and see Desgin Bureau projects on the shelves, it is a great satisfaction. The supermarket is the gallery of our work and at the same time I used to take regarding of the actual design, of design is working in stores and on the streets." (González, 2004)

"We like delivering us with passion and dedication to each project, knowing that it is an opportunity of transcending in this great playground that is creating"

Jorge Reyes Villalobos

Jota Erre Diseñadores

Mexico City, source of information: *a! Diseño* Magazine. The strategic value of design in business. B· bible 34 percent increase in sales. Interview with Jorge Reyes Villalobos. Case Study "Yoghurt B· bible Alpura."

Information and company profile

"What is the name of the office?"
"*Jota Erre Diseñadores.*"
"What is the philosophy of the office?"
"We like delivering us with passion and dedication to each project, knowing that it is an opportunity of transcending in this great playground that is creating."
"What is your mission?"
"Conformed by a human and technical team we are dedicated to resolving the graphics needs presented to us."
"What is your vision?"
"With over 25 years of experience in the field of consumer products, continue to participate in large projects for important companies."
"What is your age?"
"Now 19 years old. In 1988 was founded *Jota Erre Diseñadores*."
"What is your number of personnel?"
-Data not specified.-

Requirements of the design project

"What is the name of the study project?"

"Yoghurt B· bible Alpura."

"What was the objective of the project?"

"Alpura, leading brand in the field of dairy products, always at the forefront, he decided to change the packaging for product: drinking yoghurt Alpura."

"What was the method used to achieve the project?"

"By contacting the brand Alpura."

"What is the project concept?"

"Packaging design and product identity. Since the origin of this new bottle project would have a much more dynamic, ergonomic and contemporary design, to compete with other brands in this segment."

"What was the factor that caused the project?"

"Change the format labeling an envelope paper label to a heat shrinkable. The product would need dynamic graphics and a unique identity."

"Who developed the project requirements?"

"*Jota Erre Diseñadores* was commissioned to collaborate on this project, and besides design, suggested the *bebible* [drinkable] generic description to generate the identity of 'B· bible' and thus effectively position the product in the consumer's mind."

"Who suggested the general concept?"

"After defining the name, the logo for the brand *B· bible* developed, a logo that could be identified with a very broad target since the product goes virtually consumers of all ages."

"Who defined the final concept?"

"Another point was to develop a color code for taste since like that the product is separated from other brands in its category, on the shelf the consumer could distinguish the brand by the range of colors and flavors. The illustrations of the labels were made, to denote more 'taste appeal' in relation to the fruit to the front of the label, greater movement and weight in the front elements it gives the feeling of freshness in the image."

"Was there external support in realization of the project?"

"Not."

"How many regular meetings were?"
-Data not specified.-
"How long did the design process?"
-Data not specified.-

Project evaluation

"The briefing was considered as a strategy in business design?"
"Yes, to translate creativity and develop from the brand name to label design."
"To promote the design profession was conducive to maintaining a differential advantage?"
"Yes. With my experience as director of design at Design Associates, Walter Landor Mexico, and San Francisco, among other offices."
"What activity highlighted for greater visibility, presence and penetration for this project in the design industry?"
"It was the first project. The creation of the image that would give life to our professional success: squirrel Barcel."
"Philosophy of the firm was emphasized to explain the concept of the project?"
"Yes, give ourselves with passion to the project from the beginning to the end."
"Managers gave due importance to the brief?"
"Yes, they were shown how it's done and then accepted it with flexibility."
"The company considered design as a differential advantage?"
"Yes. Mainly brands such as Kleenex, Saba, Sangría Señorial, and all have distinguished since the creation of *Maguito de Sonrics* [Sonric's little wizard]."
"The client appreciated the advantages that professional design services bring to your company?"
"They knew beforehand, and were aware that the task would be a long process but successful."
"Was it successful project outcome?"
"Design implementation resulted in real terms, in a increase in sales of Yoghurt *B·Bible* Alpura 34% from 2005 to 2006." (Villalobos, 2007)

"It was necessary to communicate that we are experts specializing in design consulting, dare not would not have been improved the design and entrepreneurs have imagined that everything had solved. The perception changed when they saw the results"

Rafael Treviño

TD2

Mexico City, source of information: *a! Diseño* Magazine. a! Diseño-Canon Awards 2005. Interview with Rafael Treviño. Case Study "The Branding Show Image."

Information and company profile

"What is the name of the office?"
"TD2."
"What is the philosophy of the office?"
"Promote efficiency of design throughout project with communication strategies and fostering loyalty to the firm, the customer, and the consumer."
"What is your mission?"
"Carry out projects with the certainty of improving the level of design and visual communication on business adding to this, value."
"What is your vision?"
"Be positioned at the highest levels of the design Guild thanks to the delivery of our team."
"What is your age?"
"21 years. We started in 1986."
"What is your number of personnel?"
"12 members."

Requirements of the design project

"What is the name of the study project?"

"The Branding Show Image."

"What was the objective of the project?"

"This event has been developed with the purpose of transmitting knowledge, achievements, and experiences of companies that have used the branding as a tool for growth and consolidation in the companies through strategies and tactics oriented to brand, making it stronger and thus generating a functional, emotional and financial value, which promotes consumer loyalty."

"What was the method used to achieve the project?"

"It was an event in which TD2 participates as exhibitor, being our initiative can design the overall image of the event."

"What is the project concept?"

"Redesign and global communication image."

"What was the factor that caused the project?"

"In the past the image had not been as effective in their communication and seemed an event among many, as an image made in Power Point."

"Who developed the project requirements?"

"TD2. The name is already solved: Branding Show. The next step was to design a phrase that encompasses the concept of the event."

"Who suggested the general concept?"

"TD2. After several proposals, was: "The art of cultivating meaningful relationships between your brand and the consumer"."

"Who defined the final concept?"

"TD2. Once accepted phrase we started sketching and try to represent the consumer from its most primitive form and to the most complex, and came to the conclusion that the most effective way was through a signaling type person, trying to focus on the origin markings or "brands" where effectively, ranchers marked cattle with initials or very simple shapes. We frame the R in a heart, evoking even more the meaning of the phrase."

"Was there external support in realization of the project?"

"No. The client had a lot of knowledge and experience in marketing events, because they publish a magazine entitled *Merca2.0*, but did not have the expertise of a consultancy specialized on brandiing, being that the event is merited."

"How many regular meetings were?"
-Data not specified.-
"How long did the design process?"
-Data not specified.-

Project evaluation

"The briefing was considered as a strategy in business design?"
"Yes in general for project conception."
"To promote the design profession was conducive to maintaining a differential advantage?"
"It was necessary to communicate that we are experts specializing in design consulting, dare not would not have been improved the design and entrepreneurs have imagined that everything had solved. The perception changed when they saw the results."
"What activity highlighted for greater visibility, presence and penetration for this project in the design industry?"
"We did everything we needed; we seek the opportunity of business, we argue about and our customers well accepted."
"Philosophy of the firm was emphasized to explain the concept of the project?"
"Highlight the reasons why the design was necessary and to what would be reflected and the way we work."
"Managers gave due importance to the brief?"
"Yes, they were very open, and being pioneers in this kind of concept, was ample freedom for graphic development retaining the attributes of the main brand."
"The company considered design as a differential advantage?"
"Yes, more when he saw the results."
"The client appreciated the advantages that professional design services bring to your company?"
"The identity designed, transmits the focus of the event and confident to invest their money in it were felt, said customer."
"Was it successful project outcome?"
"Some participants mentioned they perceive the event, 'more professional and focused than ever'." (Treviño, 2006)

With only administration you see a glass half empty, add marketing and see a glass half full, and when you go for more water, you decided to add design. Seeing that breaks the camel, it is that it has an effect

Conclusions

About the design project management process

For a company to have an efficient development in the realization of a project should highlight different aspects of using the design projects management process:

First, on how to project their administration

1. With regard to information and company profile:

That gives rise to the search for appropriate project based on its limits on business. It shows how a company should be focused on one or more areas of design performance and how to determine the extent of business that will play according their objectives.

It is important to stress that each company should specialize in the area of design performance that is most relevant on the basis his mission, and that each project will demand different formulations depending on their qualities to develop, so each company is responsible for determining their level of skills, which will play according to the requirements of each project, so as to achieve an outstanding parameter that shows in both project and

company, its qualities. In general, you can select the projects in three specific areas:
a) Projects targeting one area of performance.
b) Projects that display various areas of design.
c) Projects supported in the development of global communication.

That reason makes companies focus their design strategies to create a project for a single product with specific qualities, or apply the consistent conditions of a specific design project in several products, or rather to develop a project with an overall communication strategy aimed at the entire context of determined products and services.

Anyway, the extent of these design strategies in each company, should always seek the highest quality parameter, on which its market reach:
a) Must not be seen as limited to one type of projects but rather as dominant in that specialty.
b) Neither as short of market share, but as project which loading of values to one market.
c) Or as an effect integrated into a process, but as a robust and integrated business strategy.

Where the importance of implementing the strategy of the company is reflected, as their formulas are based on having optimal results: of marketing, in the consumer, and for internationalize.

The study suggests that design companies project their administration (their goals, which determines the profile of the company reflects its structural strength and shows its projection to the market) into two guidelines leading to the same end, with three points each:

First: In their own development (which changes on long lasting periods) since they project their administration by tapping with its design strategy for a long period with which make recognize them by their customers:
1. To get each right project according to their profile.
2. To test the performance its structural strength in the design their own project aimed at their target customers, reflecting its own translation requirements.
3. When measure the projection to the market their own results to achieve important accounts and improve performance.

Second: In the development of the company requires their services (That change with each new project) because they adapt their design strategy during each project for making recognize their customers:

1. To direct the project according to the objectives of the company, reflecting on them their own strategies, monitoring progress, and meeting the process.
2. To carry out the project design as the market research company, putting his characteristic stamp to move the market.
3. And finally for the analysis of project results of the company in the market, in order to ensure the realization of a new project with them.

(Where the posture of his administration is highlighted and marketing and design is reflected.)

Second, on how they make use of brief

2. Regarding the drafting of project requirements (the briefing):

Summarizing the detailed information extracted from market research and contains specific requirements that the project requires. Should encourage rapprochement between those responsible for project performance and the client, for example a corporate, in a deal B2B (Business to Business); also among those responsible for the project and the final consumer when it directs it directly in a deal B2C (Business to Consumer). Its proper translation will make which are best developed the guidelines that the product requires, the briefing need precise wording and constant attention by professionals in marketing and design to build well and determine a good brand positioning, and the product in market.

It should be noted that the attention that companies will have to devote to filling the briefing is thorough, with members of his team, all involved and in all upcoming meetings; monitoring that designers should give the briefing along the project is which invites to support in its realization, first, in a B2B to the managers to achieve a correct process when are involving them to participate; and on the other, in a B2C, to involve as much as possible the responsibilities of each team member. Give seriousness and importance to the concepts of each project, such as design fundamentals and business strategies, causes maintain a formal structure based on the presence of design. In this regard, is that two aspects are dynamically cared, one is the proper integration of requirements and other improvements to the business performance of the company:

    a) With the client briefing.
    b) With the briefing of the company.

c) With briefing, customer and company.

Whereby it is noteworthy that every company should use their briefing for each project. This notice immediately that in the design is reloaded the strategy and to follow it properly it will be formed consistently, because although it has worked previously with the same client or to the same segment, it should be noted every aspect and specific guideline of the new study to clearly define a strategy.

As a result of the coexistence between company and client or company and consumer, should generate a link, the care the greatest common goal, which is the success of the project, through fulfilling of objectives that must lead to:

a) Emphasize that knowledge of the proper use of forms and visual messages excited through design.

b) Leave firmly understood that design is a valuable strategy in business which largely determines the purchase of a product or service.

c) Getting the consumer buying decision.

In which appears the relevance of the results of market research and leads the project toward its evaluation where the effects of its implementation take place in the consumer.

Plus they use the brief as a faithful tool of this process which ensures data from market research, and it is essential for each design project with which it is possible to transmit the ideal characteristics that requires the product; the study notes that one of the main reasons for the success of a project is the interest and commitment shown by managers to the design, especially when they work in drafting the brief, since a greater understanding of translation required for the project by managers, increases in them:

1. The assessment of this vital instrument.
2. The seriousness that requires professional translation.
3. The importance of preferences of the target audience.

Converting to briefing into an indispensable indicator of product taken from the point of view of the final consumer.

Knowledge that is disseminated to the managerial environment of various companies who request these services when their managers move from one company to another, leaving teachings to his subordinates and exchanged and shared between their professionals insights and feedback from projects that have led.

While much of the managers give due importance to the brief and understand that their role is essential in performing any design project, the results suggest the need to increase awareness of the use of brief among managers, even those companies that have effectively used and considered that this contributed positively to the success of your project. Whenever the brief is a tool for constant change regarding how that translates different information for each new project.

(Where the proposal of his design is highlighted and administration and marketing is reflected).

Third, on determining whether the project was successful

3. Regarding the assessment of the design project:

Highlighting the result of the realization of a project and whether it was successful to the placing on the market. This point shows that a project to be fully structured must be measured, specifically from consumer preference, to thus determine if its overall construction has had the proper effect. Effect that is manifested in management, marketing and design in action is present in the important moments of truth, that according to (Lecinski, 2011) they need of the stimulus, or exposure of the result of work that projects the product designed and promise the attributes to the prospect; and are: the zero moment: when the prospect recognizes a need and is reportedly on social media about a potential purchase. First moment: when confronting with the product on shelf and may decide to purchase. And second moment: when consuming the product and experience the pre purchase promises. Next to that according to (Cohen, 2013) is the third moment: when post-use of the product the customer becomes a true fan. This is where the aforementioned effect, which may well be called Sunrise Effect as a result of the joint work of the three main disciplines in business, it appears on the scene, with the intention of accompanying a prospectus, up in their mind, get their purchase decision and become them in a consumer.

In general, the companies surveyed say the project was successfully completed for several reasons, firstly because they and the client are pleased and are satisfied with the result of design; also highlight the difference between the previous design and the final result of the new

design; and on the other hand, are the offices that reveal the increase in the percentage of sales in the product. Three different levels of evaluation of which are the best the rate at which the consumer is satisfied. The fact is that products should be:
 a) Of high consumption that have market presence.
 b) That serves as a benchmark for competition.
 c) Than representing the image that identifies the lifestyle of a consumer, framed important situations in the lifestyle of society and issue visual formulations to awaken the constants emotions of consumer at a given time and place.

Importantly, both the factor that causes the project to be to increase sales, reposition the brand or launch a product, as the method used to get the project to be in pursuit of the project, recommendation for a project or for a specific loyalty; are a key point of differentiation, which are supported in how innovation strategies are projected as OECD (2005) says: organizational, market, product and process. These are reflected in the company's stance towards the market, the path and the portfolio, and are manifested in the mission of a company to realize a project.

So it when the companies argue that was successful the project outcome, it must be because:
 a) It is approved by the client after having shared monitoring the design process through the use of briefing.
 b) The parameters of the client, who expecting a considerable improvement in the new image of their product, are not only achieved but exceeded.
 c) The project is conducted under strict business processes supported by three main disciplines that ultimately make the difference in consumer preference.

From where excels the importance of managing the briefing, leading to the brand and the product to participate in the effect that causes in the consumer; for its consideration the determining moment of purchase.

That job of convincing between company-customer (B2B) and the development of a project to bring it to the consumer is the same then moves between client-consumer when the product is brought to market. The same whit the direct plane between company-consumer (B2C) when requesting project requirements are met and those demanded by the consumer. Convincing transmitted between design-consumer, where design largely collaborates to achieve the right effect, as a result of administration, marketing, and design working in unison at moment of purchase.

The results reveal that to ensure effectiveness in the realization of a design project is essential make a proper use of design projects management process; for planted in the sector the mission, vision and philosophy is projected; for understand and translate the information from the study or market research is required be based on the guidelines of the briefing; to achieve consumer preference everything indicates that the development an innovative proposal of design that provides emotional benefits through functional attributes and aesthetic characteristics, is what largely once put the product on the market, determines the purchase.

(Where the approach of his marketing is highlighted and design and management is reflected).

About the main commercial disciplines for success in business

So it by highlighting that this structure three sections of the design project management process proposed by Bruce et al. (1999), shows a suitable construction, one, to define the strategic strength of a company, two, to project work that will compete in the market, and three, to react with innovations to consumer demands. It is evident that this process is supported in three main commercial disciplines that are simultaneously projected in its complete development in order to ensure the success of overall project business.

These three main disciplines, that is, administration, marketing, and design, which as we have observed they stand for cause and achieve success in business being directly articulated to the development of these three parts of the above process, they can encompass as those that conform the general business process of a company.

Since they are jointly those developing the tasks that a company makes to achieve success in business as they offer, which offer, how to properly run a company so that it has a strong structure that is needed to stay in business, how develop the commercialization skills to be accepted a greater extent by the target market, and how to achieve all the qualities of communication with the expected effect the consumer chooses. And they are the activities that every company should and must do to succeed in business.

The study serves to underline that, in general, administration, marketing, and design, they can be regarded the three main disciplines in the design project management process and in the whole process of business management, to lead to success a company. Since these disciplines always act together in developing business at serve main footholds to perform the activities of business: in the company, in the market, and on the product, to finally be welcomed by the consumer.

a) When in the development of information and profile of the company (part of the business plan), they are based on management for projection as a company.

b) When in developing the drafting of project requirements (the briefing), are based on the design, to give visual prominence to a product.

c) When developing the design project evaluation, based on marketing to define the impact disseminated in the market.

Under a line of action in harmony. As the results described their behavior indicated (as a reflect of market research).

That is, they can be regarded as pillars supporting a company in any business activity. What it manifests its undeniable importance in the commercial sector, which make possible the dynamism that keeps alive the mobility between business, market, and product to take effect on the consumer, and maintain at the top to a company when they are appropriately applied.

Process that Design Companies constantly running to project its strategic objectives, to extend its scope to market, and to manage their strategies in each project achieved.

The results of this study indicate that the effective use of design projects management process converges in a better appreciation of design as a strategy of differentiation in the market and the proper use of brief results in a product well made that can fill a better effect on the mind of the consumer reflected on their preference and the increase in sales.

Therefore, it is possible to consider that know the methods of management companies design and how design is applied for large corporate in these types of companies, increase knowledge in designers and primarily in managers of large companies on how they should manage and use design.

Finding the key point with which small companies could increase the knowledge of design, as affirmed the study by Bruce et al. (1999) where it is revealed that small companies need to increase awareness of design.

Also, and which could be improved the methods of design management to increase the business impact that can generate investment in design, as pointed the study of Iduarte & Zarza (2004) which it is stated that should improve the methods of administration of design in MSMEs.

Not only with the management of design project management process, and the proper use of the briefing, but also the panorama of joint work of management, marketing, and design, as the overall business process.

Bibliography

1. Betanzos, R. (2008, June 18). Case Study "Product Catalog Philips Consumer Electronics" Figura 7 Despacho Creativo. *Design Management in Design Companies of Mexico City*. (A. Flores, Interviewer) Mexico City, Mexico. Retrieved from http://www.figura7.com
2. Bruce, M., Cooper, R., & Vazquez, D. (1999). *Effective design management for small businesses* (Vol. 20). Manchester, United Kingdom: Design Studies.
3. Charles Creel, M. (2008, May 29). Case Study "Fuerte y Claro internal newspaper Mexicana Airlines" Soluciones de Comunicación. *Design Management in Design Companies of Mexico City*. (A. Flores, Interviewer) Mexico City, Mexico. Retrieved from http://www.sol-com.com
4. Cohen, H. (2013, June 27). *Marketing: The 4 Moments of Truth [Chart]*. (L. Aronson, Editor, WebFaction, Producer, & Aweber) Retrieved December 01, 2014, from Marketing's 4 moments of truth defined: http://heidicohen.com/marketing-the-4-moments-of-truth-chart/#sthash.qaOHhTYb.dpuf
5. Espinosa, R. (2008, June 13). Case Study "Enrique Covarrubias Portfolio" 3indesign. *Design Management in Design Companies of Mexico City*. (A. Flores, Interviewer) Mexico City, Mexico. Retrieved from http://www.3indesign.com
6. González, C. (2004, February 14). Design Bureau. Entrevista a Carlos González Nacif [Design Bureau. Interview with Carlos González Nacif]. (A. Pérez Iragorri, Ed.) *a! Diseño*(67), 41-47. Retrieved september 16, 2008, from http://www.a.com.mx
7. Iduarte, J., & Zarza, M. (2004). *La administración del diseño en micro pequeñas y medianas empresas mexicanas [The design management in micro small and medium Mexican companies]*. Autonomous University of Estado de México, Faculty of Architecture and Design. Toluca: UAEM. Retrieved July 10, 2006, from http://www.dis.uia.mx/conference/2005/HTMs-PDFs/AdmondelDisenoenEmpresas.pdf
8. Lecinski, J. (2011). *ZMOT Ebook: Winning the Zero Moment of Truth*. Illinois, Chicago, USA: Google Inc.
9. Moreno, M. (2008, May 28). Case Study "Catalog Hotels Fiesta

Rewards Platinum members" Dimensión. *Design Management in Design Companies of Mexico City*. (A. Flores, Interviewer) Mexico City, Mexico. Retrieved from http://www.dimension.com.mx

10.   Muñoz, P. (2008, September 13). Case Study "Annual report of social responsibility. Mexican Coke Industry" X Design. *Design Management in Design Companies of Mexico City*. (A. Flores, Interviewer) Mexico City, Mexico. Retrieved from http://www.xdesign.com.mx

11.   Peralta, R. (2008, September 11). Case Study "Campaign fusion LexisNexis and Dofiscal" Carbono Consultores. *Design Management in Design Companies of Mexico City*. (A. Flores, Interviewer) Mexico City, Mexico. Retrieved from http://www.carbono.com.mx

12.   Pulido, J. (2008, June 22). Case Study "Napkins Pétalo Independence day" Diseño y Publicidad Mexicana. *Design Management in Design Companies of Mexico City*. (A. Flores, Interviewer) Mexico City, Mexico. Retrieved from http://www.dypm.com.mx

13.   Saavedra, E. (2008, May 11). Case Study "Karat Vodka" Sol Consultores. *Design Management in Design Companies of Mexico City*. (A. Flores, Interviewer) Mexico City, Mexico. Retrieved from http://www.solconsultores.com.mx

14.   Santiago, E. (2008, May 21). Case Study "Jafra catalog Opportunities" Ysunza Santiago Comunicación Visual. *Design Management in Design Companies of Mexico City*. (A. Flores, Interviewer) Mexico City, Mexico. Retrieved from http://www.ysunzasantiago.com

15.   Treviño, R. (2006, March 21). Premio a! Diseño-Canon 2005 [a! Diseño-Canon Award 2005]. (A. P. Iragorri, Ed.) *a! Diseño*(77), 26-67. Retrieved March 24, 2008, from http://www.a.com.mx

16.   Villalobos, J. R. (2007, September 20). El valor estratégico del diseño en los negocios. B-bible 34 por ciento de incremento en ventas [The strategic value of design in business. B-bible 34 percent increase in sales]. (A. P. Iragorri, Ed.) *a! Diseño*(86), 52,53. Retrieved September 08, 2008, from http://www.a.com.mx

www.ingramcontent.com/pod-product-compliance
Lightning Source LLC
Chambersburg PA
CBHW070331190526
45169CB00005B/1842